Da Barefoot
Warrior
of Molokai

Da Barefoot Warrior of Molokai

Soul of the Hawaiian Man

Wahine Puaa

To order additional copies of this book, contact:
Xlibris Corporation
1-888-795-4274
www.Xlibris.com
Orders@Xlibris.com
68993

CONTENTS

Dedication

I am dedicating my book of poems to my children: William Jr., Ernest, Tammy and Charmaine as well as to my hanai sons: Stanley, Ziggy and Tony. My wish for you is that you live life to the fullest and that you are happy. Life is too short! The greatest wish our Lord has is for all His children to grow in Him with the knowledge and understanding of His love. Have you ever seen a rainbow on a sunny day? I have. It only brings you LOVE! You are the best that I have ever had in this life. You are my journey. Thank you for your encouragement and for believing in me. Most of all, thank you for choosing me to be your mother! I love you . . .

Acknowledgements

With special thanks:

To my granddaughter, Charlene M. Magbaleta, for bearing the load of my poems and getting them ready for the deadline. Without your deep and faithful commitment and love this book might never have been completed. From the bottom of my heart I love you and thank you very much.

To Keola Beamer, thank you for stopping by and reading my poems. Your opinions and your warm wishes mean a lot to me. I also would like to dedicate this book of poems to mother Winona Beamer who has done wonderful things during her lifetime here in Hawaii. I wish our Alii a warm aloha on her journey home.

To my ancestors: I love you and thank you for always being with me. I thank you for all the encouragement and guidance with the unconditional love you have for me.

To the unihipili: I love you and thank you with all my heart for all the wisdom and knowledge with the understanding of who I am and for teaching me to have patience and to be humble to myself.

To my Lord, with grace and love, I thank you. Bless all those who read this book of poems. Please give them the ability to understand the spirit of aloha in their journey through my book of poems.

To my son, Da Barefoot Warrior of Molokai, Soul Of Da Hawaiian Man, aka Ernest Ka'anohiulakala Puaa: Thank you for being the keeper of your mother's poems. May the music you sing heal every heart and soul. Thank you for your love and the sweet music that heals both dad and me . . . Thank you, Lisa, for your support.

55 & Still Alive

Well here I am
55 & still alive
Still going strong
Where do you think I should be
55 & still alive
Making sure things are okay
55 & still alive
Working hard to stay alive
55 & still alive
Going to be here
As long as the Lord needs me
55 & still alive
When the time is right
I'll meet my Lord
55 & still alive
I have a lot to live for
Staying alive is one of them
55 & still alive
Hanging on by the threads
Won't let go until it's time
55 & still alive
Yes, I am staying alive
I am happy to be here
Thank you, Lord

A Journey To A Friend's House

There she was sitting and working in her yard
What a wonderful sight to see someone
You haven't seen over 20 years
The face so full of love and concern
The love for her God, Jehovah
The peace she holds with in herself
The sharing, caring for others
Opening her heart and arms
So big that she catches the one falling
And tries to put them back together again
By feeding them the spirit of aloha
And how her God, Jehovah
Loves you and waiting on you to come home
So he can take care of you . . .
Peace, joy, happiness, but above all
Is his LOVE, for his people
My thought at this moment
Could "Jehovah God, be a Hawaiian?"
So gentle, humble, warm, freedom with PEACE

A Magical Moment

wonderful things that happen by a special power

Not one sound the birds watching
At the pond how slowly in the gray colors
Mix somewhat blue with white
The soft spirit walk out of the path
Showed itself to me my heart so still watching
Asking go to her and protect her
The keiki wahine tossing and turning
Trying to make some kind of choice
Mama Kahala, came with the spirit of aloha
And said to the mo'opuna keiki wahine
A'ole pilikia [not to worry]
KeAkua showed you a path
Take a deep breath and see
I am with you always and forever
Feel the spirit inside of you
Your children is happy your circle
Is together again
The wandering spirit of Molokai is home
The ocean and the wind has come to peace
Mama Kahala, her hair in an up style with a smile
The journey comes to an end for awhile
I love you baby Kahala
Me Ke Aloha Pumehana
The morning so still
The palm trees holding its breath
KAHALA IS HOME!

A Special Place

A mother's heart
Is the most wonderful
Place to be part of

The memories that it holds
Can never leave you

This is where I keep you
This is where I hold you

This is where I tell you
How much we love you

This is where I tell you
We are so proud of you

This is where I tell you
No one can take this away from me

This is where I tell you
Thank you, my son
For choosing me as

Your mother

Are We So Blind

Are we so blind
They're standing right there
Don't we even care
To say hello, I want to meet you

Are we so blind
The hurt on their face
The smile is all broken
The wish they could run

Are we so blind
Walk away no one will miss me
Wait, I want you to meet
Too late she left

Are we so blind
To know you hurt the most
Important person in your life

Are we so blind
A tear running down her face
Feeling left out
Don't fit in

Are we so blind
The circle block
Oops! I forgot their name
Please forgive me
And I forgive you

I had to leave . . .

"Aunty Ipo"

The Queen of all Queens
The Alii of many yesterday
The love she has for her
Molokai people
How proud she was of many
Alii after her
Royalty is in her blood
For over 35 years
She has kept all
The royal court together
She was the mother Queen
Who carefully watch over us
We will never find another to
Take her place
For Molokai only has one Queen
"Aunty Ipo"
The mother Queen
Of the Aloha Week for the
Island of Molokai
Hail to the Queen
With much aloha and love
We the people of Molokai
Thank you, Aunty Ipo
As for me, I thank you with all my heart
I never know how much you mean
To me until now
I wish you
A happy journey of "Peace"
To KeAkua hale
O ka maluhia no me oe'
(Peace be with you)
May the rainbow shine on your path
May our dear father be at
The door waiting for you
Seal with the Spirit of Aloha . . .

Da Barefoot Warrior of Molokai

Barefoot Warrior,
Hawaiian Man with the spirit of aloha.
Standing tall and big
With his music to comfort all his people.

They come from the east and the west by the canoes
They carry the light of the rainbow to shine upon his path.
The love of the night rainbow, who protects him.
KeAkua, who bless everything in his path.

Da Barefoot Warrior,
Hawaiian Man, to teach the process of ho'oponopono,
So his people can find their way home.
The light of the rainbow is his only guide and
The music he sings will carry them across.

Da Hawaiian Man, Barefoot Warrior,
Is the one you can place your trust.
For he is the spirit of aloha,
From Moloka'i, Maui, Oahu, Hawaii.

Da Barefoot Warrior,
Hawaiian Man,
A man of peace, love, and joy.

Aloha, with love, to "Da Barefoot Warrior"
and "Da Hawaiian Man"
AKA Braddah Ernest Puaa,
my son.

Da Journey

Pack my bags choose carefully
What you bring because packing is an important ritual
Take along some humility, lesson of the past,
Toss in some curiosity and excitement about what you
haven't learned. Say your good byes to those
you're leaving behind. Don't worry who you will meet
or where you will go. The way has been prepared.
The people you are to meet will be expecting you.
A journey has begun. Let it be happening.
Let it unfold. All parts of the journey are sacred.
You must remember the blue print of your life is already drawn out.
Take time now to honor the beginning.
Peace on your journey home.

Da Soul Of The Hawaiian Man

He played his music with all his heart and soul
He send his music into the night
The night rainbow his ancestors helping

Carrying his melody to the island of
Molokai where his baby sister live
To tell her I love you, please forgive me

My journey was block
My heart cries out why
There is a reason for everything

Tonight as I look over to Molokai
Da soul of the Hawaiian Man
He finally sings his songs of mele

Only love for his baby sister, Charmaine
The beautiful bride of Molokai
Who married a Hilo man

The night rainbow will always protect
Da soul of the Hawaiian Man for he is
"Da Barefoot Warrior of Molokai"
Peace, faith, humble, above all LOVE

Did You Know

Did you know
WAHINEIKAWAIOLAAKANE
Was my given name
Did you know
I was born November 29, 1945
Did you know
My grandmother Rebecca
Raised my two brothers and my sister and i
Did you know
She is from the island of Hawaii in Kailua Kona
Did you know
The best time of my life was living in Waikiki
Did you know
I use to sell newspapers for $0.10
Did you know
I use to shine shoes for $0.25
Did you know
I met a Moloka'i Man
Did you know
I married him on October 17, 1964
Did you know
After 45 years I'm still here
Did you know
I LOVE MY LORD, JEHOVAH

Do The Opposite

As my kids were growing up
I said to them take a good look at your parents
If they don't look like they are making it right
Do the opposite
Life only gets one shot
If you miss the opening
The door will close and we are left behind
Do the opposite
I waited so long now I am stuck
Look at me, things just don't look right
I don't have no one to blame except myself
I gave my power away
Do the opposite
I tried to stay and make things workout
I need to take my power back
I am responsible for myself
Do the opposite
Unforgivable is living in the past
Forgive all of them and move on
For the opposite is the way out
My dreams and my life will have the chance to grow
Doing the opposite is the answer when things don't look right
Today I am 62 years old
Please don't wait that long

Embrace The Silent

A loving spirit was present
The glowing of the night and its peace
As it whisper in the wind
Telling you it's okay, you are safe
With the night rainbow shining
Upon the ocean and the waves
Dancing on the sand
The gentle touch the feeling of peace within
A tear of love and joy rolling down my face
The warmth of my heart
The music that is playing
The rainbow of the night opens up the heaven
And the glow of the heaven shining upon the
Sea shore my guardian angel at the end of the
Rainbow gently embraces me with a smile
Everything will be just fine
Mana'o i'o, to have faith, trust and believe
That, LOVE will set you free

Families Are Forever

People who you love
Never leave you

Memories is for life
Life is a freedom

Freedom is unconditional
No attachment, no aka cord

Peace is with you!

Freedom From Within

I am in all of you
Stay together
Remember everything
Then do the opposite
Love yourself first, last & always
Because I do
I was there at the beginning
And I will be there at the end
Everything I gave so freely
Only right
Everything returns to me.

Helen, From Canada

Once a year she pass by
Every moment is the same
As though she never left
What a wonderful feeling
To have with someone who
Just stop by once a year

Helen, from Canada, my friend
You are very special
May the journey you go on be bless
The rainbow smile on your path
The energy from the rainbow be your guide
Thank you, for this connection

Until we meet again
In that year you pass by
My spirit of ALOHA,
FRIENDS!

I'm So Tired

Please forgive me
I'm so tired
Wake up so early
Had to drive back
And back again

Please forgive me
I'm so tired
Running out of gas
I had to sleep
Where are you
In the park across
The street

Please forgive me
I'm so tired
I'll be there at
5:30 p.m.

Please forgive me
I'm so tired
I'll forgive you too!

Just My Imagination

In the gray mist I saw them
Standing so strong and proud
Not a smile on their faces
The image of yesterday
The hope of tomorrow
The freedom
The love for his people

They came to give me answers
Of things that was happening
I stood there gathering all

The responsibility so great
Can't let it go must stay with it
The movement is so great

They come in peace with direction
They come with love and concern

It was so clear
The mist that protect them
The image that let you see them
The night rainbow bring the promise
That they are very near
At home with you
The great gathering
Will take place

Kahala In The Moon Light

The door open and I am free
The evening soft purplish blue
With the ula ula (red)
A sacred color associated with royalty
All blend together

A beautiful mist over the ocean
The white sand turn into a dance floor
A beautiful dancer in the moon light
The glitter of the night shining upon her

The soft colors from the night rainbow
Smile upon her greeting her charm and beauty
The sweet music and sound
Played by "The Barefoot Warrior Of Molokai"

The palm tree also dancing with her
The ocean at peace with a soft whisper
Receiving her with tender love and care

The ballerina turns out to be a beautiful
Hawaiian hula dancer, KAHALA

Keep Molokai—Molokai

A ole pilikia. Molokai has no worries
A ole wind mill, Molokai has plenty makani
A ole pilikia, don't change Molokai
Let Molokai change you
Molokai can teach you how to be humble
Molokai can teach you how to love the aina
Molokai can teach you how to live with others
Stop don't think you don't know what is best for Molokai
Molokai knows what is best for Molokai
Become one of the people
But don't change Molokai let Molokai change you
I promise Molokai will teach you how to love her
If for some reason you had to leave her
You will never stop loving her, Molokai
Molokai in your heart forever
You will be in Molokai's heart too
Because she never forgets who lives on her island
Keep Molokai—Molokai

Keonani

(Beautiful Calling)

The beauty of heaven
Shine upon you today
She shower her beauty
Through the colors of the rainbow
The rainbow show her journey
What life has in store for her
Her smile and her eyes keep you
In a whirlpool of love
She holds your heart in her little hands
Keep you safe in her heart
Life itself welcome her with love and joy
For her life journey is to bring KeAkua's
Children home and to teach them how
Much KeAkua love each of them
Daddy's little angel a blessing in my life
Thank you Lord for giving me my
Little Angel . . .

"Kukuiokeanuenue"
The Light of the Rainbow

In a dream was a bright light with soft voice whispering
Calling out his name
The beautiful colors of the "Rainbow" appear
Showing the mana (power) protecting the chosen one
"The Light of the Rainbow" he will be called

Many will not understand the chosen one
But the chosen one will be blessed
And his work for KeAkua (Lord) will be his lifeline
He will serve his people with pride and joy

Like the eagle and the spirit of the rainbow
Will shower him with wisdom, knowledge with understanding

Only then he will walk beside
"The Barefoot Warrior" his father
The two will join and become one

THE JOURNEY BEGINS

Let Go Is Not So Easy

Cut the cord
Set it free
Freedom is free too
Too tired have to go
Stay in touch
Please don't lose me

Looking Into An Hour Glass

Time has no limits, it keeps moving
Our life has no limits, it keeps moving
We need to stay in touch
Don't wander in the dark, stay in the light
The clouds moving so fast doesn't know where to go
The ocean is waving and dancing
In the sand without a slipper
An hour glass is found
Just sitting on its side
Turn the hour glass upside down
The life in the hour glass is running
Please, help me save the sand from running
I just realize it's my life coming to its end.
Looking into an hour glass is looking into the future
Until then have a wonderful time
"Living"

Lord Please Help Me

Lord please help me
To be strong

Lord please help me
To be a good person

Lord please help me
And guide me on my journey

Lord please help me
And be with me

Lord please help me
My days ahead are dark

Lord please help me
Please don't let me go
Hold me tight

Lord please help me
Let the rainbow shine upon my path
And the journey I take to Honolulu

Lord please help me
Shield me in your arms
Under your wings

Lord, thank you
For hearing me

Mad Again

Just can't help myself
Always making someone
Mad again

Just can't help myself
Everyone knows
What is best for me

Just can't help myself
Keep quiet
Don't let them know
Something is wrong

Just can't help myself
You can't let them in

Just can't help myself
Always messing up

Just can't help myself
Who am I

Just can't help myself
Yes, I do know who I am

Mokihana

In the mist through the soft wind in her hair the smile on her face
The whisper in the air her name is Mokihana
The beautiful flower from the island of Kauai
The beautiful Mokihana dance under the moon and stars
All her Ohana shower her with love and the night rainbow shine
upon her path and said they have waited for a long time
To see Mokihana
Touch the lives around her with a special wave
A beautiful connection as she becomes the
beautiful Pahu rider in the parade
Her people cheers for their queen
Sending her with so much love and aloha,
for Mokihana has finally come to greet her people
with her grace and presence

My Foot In My Mouth

So many times we say things
It's not what it seems
Yet it turns out the opposite
Don't understand what went wrong
Try to make things right
They already made their decision
You are too negative
They don't understand
They want you to change
I am who I am
Made myself strong
So no one will step all over you
Need to keep myself strong
Don't let them change me
They don't own me
I give my power away no more
My foot in my mouth again
Only because they expect me to change
They say I love you
Yet that is not the question
Love got nothing to do with who I am
Because I never stop loving you
Here I am again
My foot in my mouth

My Grandson

The journey finally over
Mommy and Daddy
Waiting for the big day

The journey finally over
Sisters are waiting

The journey finally over
Papa and Mama

The journey finally over
Aunties and Uncles
Smiling

The journey finally over
10 lb. 8 ½ oz. 22in
It's a "BOY"
"Master Bulla Jr."
December 04, 2000

#14 Mo'opuna
Thank you, "Lord"

My Guardian Angel

I saw a bright light shining through
Somewhat like a tunnel
There he was my guardian angel
Waiting to take me home
The closer I got my heart my soul
Rushing with happiness
I waited so long and finally
I got to see that image
That tells the whole story . . .
So warm soft
I saw myself running toward the image
Just to hear a voice that sounds like music
Everything in that moment was pure love
Holding on this moment
My heart was full of joy, peace
So loving, I was shown another path of my journey
Live life to the fullest heal your soul
(Ho'oponopono) Make things right
The last journey comes to an end
For the next stop is freedom . . . HOME!

My Journey

Today is a very Special Day
One year ago we have gathered together
Right here at The Whaler's pool side.

My Journey today to gather all the people
Bring to them together
"Celebration of Life"
Let us never to forget what
Happen to all of us on 9-11

It's a time to remember, to recall
Time to talk & share our feelings
Time to come together, to heal
"Time for us to let go"

For the spirits and the souls of our loved ones and friends
Was carry out by KeAkua's angels and
Lay to rest until our Lord Jesus,
Will bring them all Home to his Hale.

I, Wahineikawaiolaakane,
I wish to ask for wisdom and knowledge for all of US.
Understanding to know the difference

At this time
I, Wahineikawaiolaakane,
Wish to ask KeAkua and Our Lord Jesus
Please forgive us for our many mistakes.

My Life In The Hour Glass

If I could make a wish
I would wish I made better choices
I would wish I stayed with the Lord
I would wish I can sing and dance

If I could make a wish
I would wish I took better care of self
I would wish for wisdom and knowledge
I would wish to have love and happiness

If I could make a wish
I would wish you and I have another chance
I would wish all my children and grandchildren
Have a chance to make a different life

If I could make a wish
I would wish for the rainbow to keep all my babies safe
I would wish for the spirit of the ohana to keep my children safe
I would wish for the night rainbow to bless my ohana and teach them

If I could make a wish
I would wish my life in the hour glass, take its time
I would wish my life in the hour glass be with peace and laughter
I would wish my life in the hour glass before I had to leave
I want to say thank you very much for everything you gave me
"JEHOVAH" my GOD, my FATHER in Jesus' name AMEN

My Lost Friend

I found my lost friend
Wondering where to go
And what to do

I am here I said
She doesn't hear me
Hello this is Jehovah calling
Please answer and return my calls

I am here waiting for you
Hurry don't worry

It will be fine
Wonder no more
Worry no more

For Jehovah God
Is my name and I am your
Father who LOVES YOU!

No One Is There

I was there for them
Now no one is there for me
What am I to do?
Here I sit and wait
No one is there for me
I call and call
No one is there for me
I was told before
Be aware of things around me
Don't lose the things I already have
I didn't listen
Now no one is there for me
I wish I didn't do all of this
Now it's too late
No one is here for me
What am I to do?
I keep asking the Lord
No one is here for me
After all the things I did for them
Hello, is anyone there for me
Yes, said the Lord
But you didn't hear me
Stay quite and listen the child within you
Is speaking can't you hear me too!
It's never too late to learn and understand
I was here all this time you just didn't hear me
Until now, my child

Reflection Of One Self

I was standing in a corner
Don't understand why
Feel so lost can't help
Don't know what to do

Reflection of one self
I need the need
Self need the need
Just don't want to hurt
Stay in the corner
Don't let anyone in
No one will understand

Reflection of one self
Move on, life won't stop
So sorry I can't help
Cause I need help too!

Self Be Still

Be still humble self
Be still hear the quiet within self
Be still kind to self
Be still strong to self
Be still love self
Be still peace with self
Be still trust self
Be still share self
Be still forgive self
Be still believe self
Only through the process
Release, Cleanse, Love
Self Be Still

Setting Our Self Free

I don't understand
Why you need to stay
What will set you free?
Why do you have the need to stay?
So many questions and no answer
How much of this
You want me to take
I have the need to go
I am afraid I will go
Before your time is up
And where will we be
Together or apart
I can't stay any more
I need to set myself free
Come on here I am
Still waiting
Sorry, I tried to wait
I have a question for you
Did you know at the end
It's still only me?

Someone Is At My Door

So tall and handsome
So slim and refreshing
Dark hair somewhat long
The eyes so round and blue
Deepest blue so soft like our
Beautiful sky when the sun
Opens its eyes and gives us the
Breath of Life to start our day
Thank you for stopping by
Farewell until we meet again

Somewhere Above The Rainbow

Somewhere above the rainbow
Only meek ones follow
Through all the tears and sorrows
There's a great tomorrow

Stay with me and we will see it through
Flying freely he cares for me and you

Somewhere beyond the horizon
Dew drops kissing morning
Rays of warmth that shines on new land
There's no fear of dying

Take my hand don't ever let go
Believe in me and I will set you free
Just keep alert and watchful
It will soon be here
I know that you will love it
Look it's almost near

Written by Marevic Gines

Soul Of Da Hawaiian Man

Have you ever seen the rainbow on a sunny day?
It appears when it's quiet on a beautiful morning
With a smile on her face shining in this beautiful day
Stretching her hands out giving tender love and care

Soul of Da Hawaiian Man gives thanks for all his blessings
The rainbow sends him a gift of love to take his place on a journey
Called life with KeAkua at his side
Kukuiokeanuenue shines the light on his path
And the journey of Ho'oponopono to help his people

Soul of Da Hawaiian Man takes his place and starts to teach
Have you ever seen the rainbow on a sunny day?
She shares her beautiful colors of ulaula (red), indigo blue
Magical emerald green that heals the soul
It promises to keep her people safe

The gift the soul of Da Hawaiian Man received
Have you ever seen the rainbow on a sunny day?
Without a doubt his gift was Ka'anohiulakala
Soul of Da Hawaiian Man smiles with joy and happiness
Thank you, KeAkua . . .

The Brave One

So many things going on
Still the faith is holding on
How do I help?
Can't because the brave one
Got it all together
Stand still and learn
Watch it all come together
Faith is all he got
Faith will carry him and his family
Over that burning bridge
The water of life will burn out the flame
And his faith will set him free
I wish I could help the brave one
But I too should have the faith
Things will turn out and set everything free
Peace, Faith and Love
Will open the door of Freedom
Then life just goes on and on
For the brave one

The Day Is Closing In

The day is closing in
No time to think
Here goes anything
Please Lord let it be okay
The day is closing in
Feeling kind of scared
Please Lord let it be okay
Made some people unhappy
Over step wasn't my intention
Please Lord let it be okay
Please Lord forgive me
And I forgive them . . . .
7, 8, 9 . . . .
Please Lord let it be okay

The Day Will Come

When I am gone
Can't be found
Only then will
They miss me

I am here now
Why do you
Take so long
To come to me

Only time will tell
I am sorry
I had to leave

Please, hurry before
We miss each other
Oops!
Hope to see you
I had to leave

The Great Choice

It was a perfect day
Everything was perfect timing
The families and special friends
The ocean was so great dancing
On the sand and smiling with joy
The great news was coming
The rain came and protects her
And stayed with her until she finished
With what she had to tell her people
The great choice was made
She told them how important they where
To her and said she will always love them
No one knows that answer
She told them she decides not to do the kidney dialysis
That she will finish her life until the Lord takes her home
Then the great rain stops right after her speech
She felt the weight was lifted
She was at peace with her inner family
She place everything in KeAkua hands
As he carried her off
I love you my ohana
Not all was happy with the choice
What about me I said it's not your call
I don't want to give my children any problems or stress
I know for a fact because I did try to take care of my folks
Don't you remember? I love you
Please forgive me and I forgive you

The Hands Of Love

She sits down to write
Her fingers so hard
The flame in her fingers
The lotion the aloe can't do the job
Sticking her hands into the sand
To cool it down the flame in her fingers
Running all over unsure how it all got started
She hold on to her hands pain so bad
Wondering what is the best thing
To heal the pain
I reach out for her hands
Softly places them into my hands
Holding so tender gently
So the crack in her hands will fade away
The spirit of the old women
The smile in her face tells the whole story . . .
She is fine and she keep moving on
Mind over the matter is a powerful tool

The Images Of Yesterday

In the gray mist I saw them
Standing so strong and proud
Not a smile on their faces
The image of yesterday
The hope of tomorrow
The freedom and love for their people

They came to give me answers
Of things that are happening
I stood there gathering all

The responsibility so great
Can't let it go must stay with it
The movement is so great

They come in peace with direction
They come with love and concern

It was so clear
The mist that protects them
The images that let you see them
The night rainbow brings the promise
That they are very near at home with you
The great gathering will take place

The Life Of The Warrior

To Love KeAkua
To Love The Son of God, Jesus Christ
To have peace within one self
To make things balance around him
To care and protect for his family
To always carry out the "Spirit of Aloha"
To walk on the path of God's Light
To talk and teach the children
To always remember {KeAkua} love you first
To keep the Ten Commandments
To remember the "Lord's Prayer"
To remember the "Rainbow" and its promise
To believe the "Night Rainbow" is true for
The old folks/ohana never leave us
To seal all things with "KeAkua" and
His son "Jesus Christ"
Then and only then, freedom to all

Written by Francis Kamakawiwaole

The Light Within

There she stands with her arms
Holding on to the heavens
Thanking her Maker for the
Beautiful sun setting

The light within His heart
Breathless to enrich your soul
The mist from the rain clears the path

The beautiful colors from the rainbow
Stretching into the four corners
Of the universe
Sending its aloha to the people of Hawaii

Malama pono O'Hawaii
KeAkua gives his light within
So you can feel the peace from the night

The Power of Peace

Peace, Peace, Peace
Love, Love, Love
Freedom from all aka cords

Before the candle lights
Before they all yell with joy
Before the tears

Within your heart
A calm place to be
Behind closed door

Just you and the Lord
One on one, one on one
Just reach and he will

Be right by your side
Making sure you are safe
Teaching you the process

To make right, to rectify
To release
To cleanse
To transmute

Offering you the wisdom
The understanding
With the knowledge
To know the difference

Until then, ka Maluhia no me oe
"PEACE, be with you"

The Pride Of Molokai

Oh! Molokai look at you
So beautiful and peaceful
I miss you Molokai
I wish I was home with you

I look across the ocean
There you are
With your green coat
Shining and flowing

With a smile on you
Greeting people from afar
Welcome, welcome
Come and sit awhile

Let's talk story
People come from afar
The four corners
Of the world

The pride of Molokai
Is with all of you

The Spirit Of Aloha, Hawaii

The people of Hawaii
The tears that flood the land
Wondering about the loss of our
Brothers and sisters
The spirit of Aloha, Hawaii
The darkest day in our life

The people of Hawaii
Wondering about the choice
Our brothers have made
Don't they know it's against KeAkua (God)?

The people of Hawaii
Calling out to you Life is too
Precious to take in your hands
The spirit of Aloha is in you
For KeAkua (God) gave it so freely

The people of Hawaii
Unfortunately time has to go on
Smile and absorb the physical being
For one day you will need to

Release your beautiful SMILE
To enjoy the memories that you have
Both shared through the years
Aloha, until we meet again

The Timing & The Blessing

It was always said timing was so important
The flow that brings the light in
Given by KeAkua
The blessing of our Lord
The special bond and connection
That made so many people
Come together as families and friends
In our life today on earth
It's so important to make things pono

"For in every tunnel has a dark side of uncertainty,
every uncertainty has a choice,
every choice has a reason,
every reason has a person,
every person has a spirit,
and every spirit has a light."

May God bless the journey we all need to go on before
We too can go home
If the path you take has a tunnel,
your spirit will have a brighter light at the end
PEACE, LOVE, and FORGIVENESS
Will forever set us FREE

Written by Ernest Puaa

The Untold Story

Life is a story someone didn't tell us no matter what goes on we are still wondering why, how come, all these things are happening don't know what to say
Life just keeps going on with or without you
Life is here to stay but not all of us are here to stay
The word life seems long but it's not what it seems
This was told to me
Everything is not what is seems
Life is another word for death
Because everything comes to an end in life
Sickness is another word for death
My end is coming soon and I ask the Lord
To please forgive me and thank you for the Life I was given

Thoughts To Release

The pass is the pass
And
I will be fine
The pass cannot hurt
Me anymore . . . .
Peace be with me
And
Peace is with the pass
This too shall pass
And
I too shall pass
Today, I release my pass
And
Ask my pass
To please forgive me
And
I too forgive you

Only through the process of
Self I-Dentity
Through Ho'oponopono
I will be free forever
Amen // Peace

What Is A Perfect Life

Put your trust in the Lord
Be humble
Be understanding
Be a good listener
Be able to share the good news about the Lord
Be gentle to the soul
So many times we tend to go out of our circle
To find the answer . . . yet we find it's not there
What is a perfect life
What is a perfect life
It's the life we pick with our Lord
The blueprint that was laid out
Before we left for our journey to earth
We had good choices we need to know
We do have a blueprint
To follow our journey
To make things in our life easier
Just keep the faith and in due time
Everything will show itself

When I Die

When I die
Love me in peace

When I die
I want you to live

When I die
Please stay alive

When I die
I live in you

When I die
I am in peace

When I die
Because of you
I live again

Who Am I

Do you know who I am
Please tell me

So many people
Know who I am

But do you know
Who I am

Please tell me
Who I am

They know what
Is best for me

Do I know
Who I am

Don't want to
Cause any problems

I don't know
Who I am
Any more

CPSIA information can be obtained
at www.ICGtesting.com
Printed in the USA
LVHW101459130622
721138LV00004B/225

9 781441 593801